Telephone Talk

by Ahmed Hassan

PEARSON

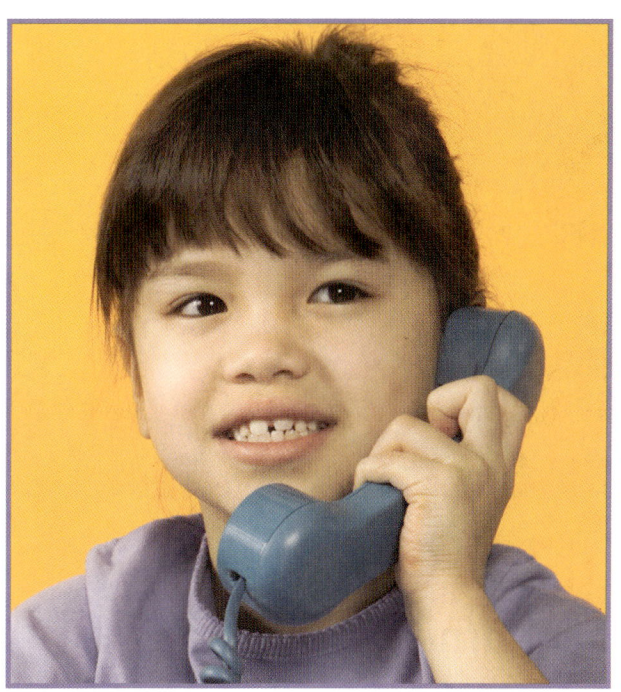

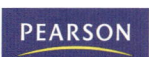

Glenview, Illinois • Boston, Massachusetts • Chandler, Arizona
Upper Saddle River, New Jersey

Let's learn about telephones.
They are also called phones.

One part is for your mouth.
One part is for your ear.

Grandma

Grandma is far away.
You can talk to her on the phone.

Some phones have cords.

Some phones do not have cords.
You can walk around with them.

Be nice when someone
uses a phone.
Do not make noise.

Telephones help us talk to people near and far.